PIECING TOGETHER

David Scott was born in 1947 in Cambridge. He was educated at Solihull School, and studied Theology at Durham and then at Cuddesdon College near Oxford. He spent two years as a curate in Harlow, and then became School Chaplain at Haberdashers' Aske's School, Elstree, where he taught religious education. He was vicar of Torpenhow and Allhallows in Cumbria for eleven years, and since 1991 has been Rector of St Lawrence with St Swithun in Winchester and Warden of the Diocesan School of Spirituality. He is an Honorary Canon of Winchester Cathedral.

In 1978 David Scott won the *Sunday Times*/BBC national poetry competition with his poem 'Kirkwall Auction Mart'. *A Quiet Gathering*, his first book of poems, was published by Bloodaxe Books in 1984, and won him the Geoffrey Faber Memorial Prize in 1986. His second collection, *Playing for England* (Bloodaxe Books, 1989) was a Poetry Book Society Recommendation. Both books were illustrated by Graham Arnold of the Brotherhood of Ruralists. The poems from the two collections are republished with new work in David Scott's *Selected Poems* (Bloodaxe Books, 1998). His latest collection is *Piecing Together* (Bloodaxe Books, 2005).

David Scott's collection of poems for children, *How Does It Feel?* was published by Blackie in 1989. He has also written several plays for the National Youth Music Theatre with Jeremy James Taylor. These include *Captain Stirrick*, which was staged at the National Theatre's Cottesloe Theatre in 1981; and *Bendigo Boswell*, which was commissioned by the BBC and screened in 1983. *Jack Spratt VC* was performed in the 1986 London International Opera Festival, and *Les Petits Rats* was performed at the Edinburgh International Festival and Sadlers Wells in 1988. He has written four religious books, *Moments of Prayer* (SPCK, 1997), *Building Common Faith* (Canterbury Press, 1997), *Sacred Tongues* (SPCK, 2001) and *The Private Prayers of Lancelot Andrewes* (SPCK, 2002).

He is married to Miggy, and they have a daughter and three sons.

David Scott

PIECING
TOGETHER

BLOODAXE BOOKS

ISBN: 1 85224 696 0

First published 2005 by
Bloodaxe Books Ltd,
Highgreen,
Tarset,
Northumberland NE48 1RP.

www.bloodaxebooks.com
For further information about Bloodaxe titles
please visit our website or write to
the above address for a catalogue.

Bloodaxe Books Ltd acknowledges
the financial assistance of
Arts Council England, North East.

Cover printing by J. Thomson Colour Printers Ltd, Glasgow.

Printed in Great Britain by
Bell & Bain Limited, Glasgow, Scotland.

for Miggy

ACKNOWLEDGEMENTS

Acknowledgements are due to the editors of the following publications in which some of these poems first appeared: *The Merton Journal, Church Times, The Southern Echo* and *The Colebrook Courier*. 'Prayer and the Hair Salon', 'The Priest in the Pulpit' and 'Resurrection' were broadcast on Radio Solent's *Morning Thought* in May 2004.

CONTENTS

First Thing

One young deer
on the path to the wood
then following
three more together.
How it stopped me
even inside the house
my shirt in my hands
every bit of my body
wired up for watching
every bit of theirs radar
for the merest blink.
Air rigid between us,
they moved first,
nobly, silently,
sensuous as waking.

This Meadow, a Soul

Left to grow beautiful
the grassy heads do gentle talking,
and as a whole move to an unseen hand,
this way and that. The size of a soul
is like this, just let to be, to breathe,
to bathe in its own space. God has every
confidence in it, resisting continual visits
to check on how it's going. It's going all right.
Occasionally a secret breath unseen
blows joy across its face
and in return the soul picks up its skirts
and makes long swathes in meadow lengths of space.

Valley Road, Louisville

Thanks be to God
that sometimes we can
walk in Eden. Quiet
in the morning, I catch
the shadow and the sun,
so neither hurt.
I know there's a world
elsewhere, but am allowed this one.
Whatever the six-fold lips
of the lily say, they say it kindly.
Trees there are in plenty
arching like Blake's tall angels
over me, each a blessing, none
bearing the troublesome apple.

The Barnes Home Guard Ground

A strictly suburban Sunday morning
means the majority are still asleep, while
I go out for the pleasure of walking,
not far mind you, hardly half a mile.
I find winter poised in the muffled freeze
of pavements. Deep in a cowl, head bent,
pure walking, occasionally I blink up
at the pollarded trees, statues with fist ends.
Between the semi's is a secret yard
which draws me between creosote fences
to the Home Guard Ground. Then it had
the whole of Barnes to defend, now
the sun fires westward at a dead tree,
making the deadness gold, quite suddenly.

Brighton Pier, 10 A.M.

It's quiet at the moment.
The chips are still their pale potato selves.
The *Brasso*'s whitening on the ornaments,
and someone's counting something on the shelves.

An early group of three, breathe
the freedom of not land, not sea.
There's no Fortune Teller in the booth.
The deckchairs, in their horizontal piles, are free.

The Galloping Steeds are motionless.
The smells of vinegar and Candy Floss
incubate in silence
anticipating their release.

With everything just that little out of reach,
I'm given space to lean against the rail,
and watch a girl tread the sliding beach,
each loping step leaving a long trail.

It was as if she'd
waited all the way from Birmingham
to lift a cupped hand of the sea,
and to cast it, randomly.

Black and White Photographs

We were staying overnight beside the Rhine
and over breakfast I kept wanting to look
more closely at the photos on the wall.
They were of the parents of the present owner,
and the Guest House with its ivy and turret
as it was in 1945.

It was her, though, who was translucent.
How is it that black and white can capture
such a perfectly ordinary saint, reminding me
of pictures of my mother in the same year,
the austerity wedding ones?

This was a work of art. It should have been titled
'The Saint that had the Guest House',
and her praises sung. Breakfast
was in the extension and the builders
that very morning were doing away with the wall
on which the pictures hung.

Mud Revisited
(for May Badman)

I was stumbling across a field
with the magazine in hand
reading the published poem. 'It was there!'
My first. What was I doing in the field?
I was ascending with the larks.
Cyclostyled and stapled, the cover
the colour of blancmange, and the poem
was there. Why should it make a difference?
It wasn't a big poem as poems go,
but I'd sent it into the great unknown,
and half forgotten about it.
What had become of the poem was anyone's guess,
but in the dark unpredictable 'no' of publishing
some unforgettable eye had said 'yes'.

Prayer and the Hair Salon

I am a priest of Winchester.
A candle flickers in the upstairs cell.
I watch the snow fall on the heads
of the passers-by. My prayer is soft
as snow. It does little but
cover the ground, and the candle shivers.

Opposite and down is a Hair Salon.
I can see the long napes of necks
as the hair is lifted, curled, and cut,
or pinned with papers like bookmarks.
I pray, and because of the cold
hug my already tight cloak tighter. Why?

Strange contradictions don't have
answers always. It happens so.
What do I pray for: that the heat
could be shared, that I should get a
haircut, that they will put down
their scissors and pray?
Not yet. Someone higher looks at me,
and says 'poor fool'; or perhaps,
'all you need to do is stay'.

The Priest in the Pulpit

Will it last, this opening of the heart
to the Word, or will the new ways,
the film, the television, the e-mail,
dislodge us from the art of oratory?
Climbing the steps, taking off the paper clip,
remembering not to put it in my mouth,
the text, the Greek, the joke, the text again,
all this, O God, you know, as well as asking you
to make all things, especially the haste,
respectable. As the spiral notebooks rust
along the shelves, who knows how a word
in the thickest of the sermon's stickiest part,
might just have winged its way into the heart
of one young stranger there, and taken roost.

Meeting St John of the Cross

I would look for signs of weather
at the edges of your clothes, your hands
for the way you hold your pen, and put it down.
I would glance to notice shifts of sun and shadow
of the alternating poetry and prose in you.
I would be curious, acute to sense
such mundane sacraments. The drawing,
small and aerial of Christ, seen
from the Father's desperate height, and the voice
which reached down songs from such tall trees,
would pose questions, as unanswerable
as why the storks so love the towers of Avila.

Augustine Baker talks to the Nuns of Cambrai

So much to say. The Cambrai days were long
and the nuns didn't have to attend,
which meant they didn't, except one,
and then one by one, until there were ones
all over Christendom. The first words though,
the early tentative drafts, the birdsong
while the hill above the trees stood still
in the mist, what of those, before they were books,
when there were only a few words and those
the same: 'silence, solitude, love, and love again'?

Caedmon's Song

Wind through the consonants,
air through the vowels,
starlight through the planks,
God in the outhouse.

That's where the poem began.
I saw it from the B & B
looking across from the barn
to the ruin of the Abbey.

Among the cattle, the air
in the silence, the wind
in the dust, I heard you
before breakfast, and made

this song of it. God
of the nearer presence
and the long view
I saw you, and I sing of you.

The Healer

I asked her what she did, and
she said, 'healer'. We talked
about the central nervous system
and how I wasn't looking after mine.
There was no grille or wooden box
but it had the air of a confessional.
The music was about to start again
which left no time for absolution
in the conventional sense. I think
she might have been an angel, for
I have the indent of a wing along my side.

For Pete Laver
(1947-1983)

After all these years
here comes the elegy.
We walked the long path from the church
to the burial ground, not quite sure
whether to talk or not. It was warm
and bright. (Twenty years on
it is drizzling).
                    You were so funny.
The first time we met, you were perusing
the headstones in our churchyard
having earlier backed your car
into the River Derwent near Wordsworth's house.

Here is your grave, the smallest of stones
like a bit off someone else's. Perhaps
someone nicked it for you, that would figure.
The lettering has almost gone so I trace it
with my finger like Braille, 1947,
we began together...

It was a warm day in summer,
so many poets, so many young people,
women in gay dresses, so much beauty
and memories of laughter. So,
why then
after all these years this
uncontrollable checking of tears?

Heart on Pilgrimage

My heart goes walking
to the ancient places,
Jerusalem, Lindisfarne,
holy places all. Prayer
can take me there:
to the foot of the cross,
to the edge of the world,
to the eye of the Buddha,
the muezzin, the kestrel
hovering over the motorway,
and my heart can go thwack
to another heart as quick
as silicon, but
bringing it back...

The Church of the Holy Sepulchre, Jerusalem

She is in love with someone, I can tell.
When she sits, she sits alone and still.
Her shrouded face, encompassing profound denials,
surfaces in light, and says, 'I will'.

Her movement speaks of shadows, edges,
and who it is she loves is not found here,
not there, but moving from the centre
of her longing, is with her everywhere.

Qumran, Cave no.4

Despite all the talk of the Prince of Light,
this is the centre of the coolest darkness.
The light which on the outside
makes a dust of stones, here only angles in,
and the scrolls rolled up in jars, sleep:
sleeping and waiting for the chance eye
of a Bedouin boy. Why now, why then:
these scrolls about so fervently
expected things, waiting, waiting?

Mea Shearim, Jerusalem

On the shutters and the crumbling walls
ripped notices, only words,
flap in the cold, late Sabbath wind.
I peep into heaven, and there
the bright neon strip-lighting
glazes the black and white Hasidim
twiddling hair and stroking beards
in the House of the Lord.

High up and diagonally across the road,
a daughter of Jerusalem
eyes her brothers through the chink
of makeshift wooden slats.
They sway and nod and say so well
the things they have to pray
on the terraced sides of heaven.
Long after her bedtime, she thinks
what is it to be a sister, a woman, a bride?

A Boat on Iona Bay

So many times my pen has tried that boat:
how she rests in the water as if nothing
could bother her; how much she enjoys just floating,
waiting release from the anchor.
The slight laying back of the masts and rigging
is very satisfactory. Happy in herself, breathing
as if she might have just been drawn
through the tight neck of a bottle, and raised
and rigged full-sail, upright.

St Columba's Bay, Iona

Among the bones of seagulls
      and of kings
and with all this muffled, nibbled turf
    even the sea's gone quiet,
        imagine that!

In respect for such unusual tenderness
      it wasn't difficult
  to walk the long way home
cradling a crab shell in my hand;

leaving behind, on this occasion
    the weight of intricate stones.
      It was with a light step
        that afternoon
        I made it home.

With Miggy at Skelwith Force

This was where my father brought me,
and now in bringing you
I sense a change in scale and clarity.

Water eases from a petrol smoothness
into a broth so fierce the rocky sides
seem moving up and not the water down.

A fish falls upwards flashing black
against the bridal veil of spume,
and at the edge a single harebell shivers.

All this meant danger for a father and a son,
but now, with he away and I grown out of sandals,
there's no longer any reaching up for rail or hand.

I know a different sort of peace,
something about holding the wonder
in a new-found capacity to understand.

Gertrude Jekyll's Lindisfarne Garden

I thought I would not know the names
but there are the sweet peas beginning
the summer climb up the bamboo sticks.
Those are daisies sealing the cracks
in the paths. Roses are in the sunny corner
with the pink rambling thing we've got at home.
The lavender's gone purple, rosemary has an ancient stem,
and the brightest things of all are crimson,
flapping poppies. I know a bench when I see one.
A sundial says it's teatime in the castle
which is a whole wide bowl of sky away
yet still in the sound of the sea. *A garden enclosed*
is my sister, my spouse: I take that as the text
that brings thin Cuthbert and such floribunda
next to each another.

A Window in Ely Cathedral

I am a window full of glass
pieced from fragments blown apart in wars
where old conjunctions and a random placing
are lit just where the sun decides to pause.

A leering bit of face with twisted lips,
a bit of beard, and letters almost spelling 'holy',
a sheaf of corn, a leaf, and then the sun dips,
lighting Mary in her simple glory.

The misplaced jigsaw rearranged in parts,
slips at the edges into bits of dream.
The sun is patient, and its darts
redeem my war-torn lack of scheme.

'the infinite sweetness of the Greek text'

SIMONE WEIL

Dear Simone, I know what you mean
but only now, at last.
I found my student text, disregarded,
naively underlined in biro.
It was the pressure of exams.
I re-read Peter's words to Jesus,
You are the Christ:
four words in Greek
but stripped of English cloy,
and shining separately bright. The Greek
spread through me like a dye,
(and would you understand this too?)
came to rest, not only through the language,
but in the precision of their being true.

Ibn Abbad woke early

Ibn Abbad woke early, put on
his patched garment, turned to God
and said, *Peace be to us, and to all, this
day.*

Rabbi Schmelke of Nikolsburg,
when a rich and distinguished man
tried to make him look ridiculous,
read the forty-first psalm, and
translated verse eleven, *By this
I know that you delight in me:
my enemy will suffer no ill because of me.*

Father Louis in his American hermitage
wrote to Abdul Aziz, *Let us
have great love for truth, and open our hearts
to the spirit of God our Lord and Father,
Compassionate and Merciful.*

All three went to Paradise,
Ibn Abbad, Rabbi Schmelke of Nikolsburg,
and Father Louis, and sat to eat
at the same table. They drank the water of life
and ate the meat of friendship. Whenever
their cups ran dry or their plates were empty
a little Nazarene came by and filled them up.
Who are you? they said.
I am Jesus, son of Mary. Can I sit awhile?
Be our guest, they said.

As they sat, the ground beneath them shook,
their faces paled and their eyes were filled
with knowledge, and with grief. *Today,*
said Jesus, *they will hate more and
love more, than on any other day since
the world began. Hold hands,
and ask our God to speak to us
in Spirit.* And there they sat

in love and prayer, all day, all day,
Ibn Abbad, Rabbi Schmelke of Nikolsburg,
Father Louis, and Jesus, Mary's son.

and their silence was more profound than words
and their communion was most eloquent
and they willed the world to peace

After a long time they opened their eyes,
and there were only three at the table.
Jesus, Mary's son, had gone,

    had gone to join some other hands in love
    sit by some other beds of pain
    pray with some other desperate men
    break for some other hearts the loaf
    share with some other faiths the way

and that goes on today
unceasing in his care to see beyond the robes
of different length, and hue, and cloth,
the common beating heart, and to mark again
as on the Bethlem night, the angels' call:
Peace on the earth, goodwill to all, to all.

The Mug

We'd seen them in the Ashmolean:
Cistercian Ware. I thought of Rievaulx,
and asked if you could make the same design:
black glaze, tallish, the waisted shape.
You did, and when you were in hospital
that was the mug I chose to sip from,
in the early hours, imagining you gone.
I turned you, and turned you, until,
putting you down beside the lamp,
I was amazed at how the black glaze shone

On thinking of not throwing the old Road Map away

I've read it upside down, right way up,
with glasses, without, driving and stationary,
marked in green felt-tip pen the way to The Dell,
via Raymond Rd, Gresham Rd, Atherley Rd,
put a red circle round the Grosvenor Square Car Park
so I could get to the Art Gallery through Watts Park.
What isn't marked, but should be, in gold,
is the boot that turned up on the side of the
Chandlers Ford by-pass just before the roundabout
leading into Bassett Avenue. It was there
like a Monopoly piece, every time we passed
on the way to the General, to watch and wait
and wonder about a brain being mended,
a life being sewn back into place. When it was,
and we went back together to the shops,
to buy curtains or some other stuff,
the boot had gone. It was there, like God,
or the surgeon, or a good friend, just long enough.

I pollarded am

I pollarded am.
My elbows ancient are,
but my hair, which
out of my neck does grow,
the head hacked off having been,
is young, absurdly, rubbery so.
O so ancient my chest and hips
pressing the legs of me, now stumps,
deep into underground.

Why do they this pollarding do?
One day, no doubt,
thus and thus did some king say.
So from the folly of an autumn cut,
it came to must be so.

They say in China this they do to feet,
in other countries, minds,
and others, souls. Thus nature rearrangèd is.
I know not what I think
not having head,
for I pollarded am.

Eyes

Eyes take in the light for hearts to see by.
They are quintessentially the mind's messengers,
barometer of the soul's weather,
and the heart's health.
We tell by the eyes. Looking is the least they do.
When eyes touch others' eyes they sign in.
When it's a stranger in a crowd, on the street,
in a train, and that's all there is of it,
I like to think they are my brother and my sister.
I like to think they are never lost.
God of the one strand of hair, are you also
God of the one look, of the glance, of the glimpse?
I trust one day all will be known
in the deepest bank of the world's meaning
and on that day our eyes will feast.

On not looking

I thought to look them into love,
the dazed, the half-crazed,
and that seemed almost everyone
on the Euston Road that afternoon
of sirens and haze.

But someone once advised me
who opened the door and
was punched to the ground
not to look them in the eye, for
it only troubles them more
apparently. Look up, look at the floor,
look all around, but not searchingly at.

So I walk on, drawing the curtain
of the soul's windows, eyes walled.
I decide to play Christ not at all,
in a fast withdrawing world.

The Old Ferry

Half in the mud, in the thick of the gulls' squabbles,
an old ferry becomes more and more
what its builders would remember. The square nails
long to be driven home. The prow
can only be imagined now. I embark,
clambering on weather-worn planks.
A child joins me with his questions:
'what is this?' and 'what is that
half-wood-half-iron thing?' We agreed
it was something to do with something else,
possibly the rudder, deep into the mud.
When the bright, new ferry arrived, the child
jumped off his friendly, timbered skeleton,
turned, waved, and called out
a strangely old-fashioned 'goodbye!'
I was left looking into history,
sensing the rain would reveal more grain,
until what once was tree, would, in time, be tree again.

Reflections on Craigie Aitchison's Paintings

1
See,
>   a leafless tree
>   leaning to the right,
>   a fingernail clipping
>   moon,
>   and Wayney being
>   sucked
>   upside down
> through a thunderous sky
>   to Heaven.

2
See,
> people smile in recognition,
>   find their friends and point.

3
See,
> the Pope walking in the garden
>   in his white soutane
>   in the human being stretch of space
>   the horizontal band of being us
>   with the trees
>   the visiting birds
>   and the round black papal hat
>   cruising in its own air space.

4
See
> the cross, but:

> Q. What is the dog doing there?
> A. Oh!
>   howling beneath the bright cross
>   his Master is shining from.

A David Jones Annunciation

In such an ordinary room
the angel came skidding to rest:
she on a bench of prayer
he to get news off his chest.

Arrivals can happen like that
on the day you least expect,
when the washing's on the line
and you've no idea what's next.

He was such a gentle angel
with a lily in his hand,
and his eyes so meekly angled
you has to understand.

The King is in search of a kingdom;
the time to be born is soon,
and God wants you to house him
in the byre of your womb.

She sat as still as the chair
staring at the cool, tiled floor
and the silence was deeper there,
than she'd ever heard before.

Neither knew how to break it.
Neither was wanting to press.
It was probably only a minute
but it felt like an hour to say 'yes'.

'Yes' was the shape of the farmhouse.
'Yes' were the trunks of the trees.
'Yes' was the gate on its hinges.
'Yes' brought the world to its knees.

A David Jones Nativity

(Gentilis animetur)

All four hooves, Welsh as a pony on hill
are inches off the frosted ground. They skip
for a fish tight saviour who is swathed in stillness
between apple breast and pillow of hair.
Come to look at it, all are off the ground:
cow and ladle, shepherdess and lute,
bits of floating Latin, but all stock still,
as if playing statues.

I am waiting for the cockerel to spill
its redness on the page to Botticelli up the colour
and set the world in motion, from out of winter
into summer. Then the snow will melt
and who knows what the sun might loose them into.

Uglow's Nudes

Looking at Uglow's nudes
in the Abbot Hall Art Gallery
what I felt was missing was
the replacing of old breath by new.

So I opened a window and looked
instead at the castle ruin, and thought
of Catherine Parr who wore so many
clothes, including a ruff. I saw a seat too
on the top of the hill and the millennium beacon.

Then I knew as before
that really good paintings
make me want to write poetry.

Playing Lutoslawski in Grasmere Church

Is tragedy suitable at any time?
Can sun or holidays lend a rhyme,
as they did today, calling us from here
to Warsaw in one long drawing of a bow?
Yes, at any time, and better
coming from a player who was born
so the programme says, way after the music.
All so young, and into youthfulness was slipped
this whisper from the camps.
In the heart of the festival and the heat,
the funeral days were back.

Pablo Casals plays to the wall

What a fine wall, ancient I would say, of a church,
and the large stone flags are alive with the light
that plays on an old man's bald head.
The head of the cello nestles his neck.
I see his back and his poise.
He plays to the wall, this man
who could fill a concert hall twice over.
He plays, then, for the joy of it, there,
where only the angels come, one
by curious one, stirring the air.

The Piper

It was the relation of bag to pipe
that interested me, like taking
a red velvet pig to market under
your arm: the constant rearrangement
of elbow and finger to accommodate this
live thing. The venue for the night,
the island's ancient lending library,
was in a frenzy. The dusty summer coals
might just have turned to fire.
It took the final tune to reveal
a face made generations ago, when
your grandfather played the same pipes.
The encore set your eyes upon some other island,
on some far distant archipelago.

The Organist's Wrists

Something has to link the brain with the music,
and I think it's the wrists. Wrists put the hands
in the right place, and are the swings for the music
to take flight up to those heart stopping heights,
and back, so your stomach is left where it was,
several feet behind your body. It's the wrists
that hold the fingers to the job, the task
of typing music into living keys.
I've seen how the wrists bring the whole service
to rest, long after the choir have ditched their
cassocks for a smoke and a pint of best.

West Malling Abbey

You know how a moving camera seems
to make the buildings move themselves,
though nothing could be more fixed.
Well, it was like that. I was walking
on a winding path and the tower
and the chapel roof began
to move around themselves, like
a model of the constellations speeded up.
The path and the river at my feet wound
round a different figure of eight,
and I became a dance within a dance,
moving to the sacred space of church.
There we made a circle round the sacrament,
and passed the kiss of peace.
Christ came round in bread and wine,
until all ceased. I could hear my breath
grow quieter in the silence of a little death.
The dance had done its thing.

The Friends' Meeting Room

I have known silences between
breaks in conversation, agonisingly
searching for the next word. I remember
the silence of exams curdling in my stomach;
and the silence of aloneness filled
with small domestic noises,
a kettle clicking off and distant traffic.

I've even known a silence bring me
to my knees, in an ancient church, held
through the regular deep ticking
of a mechanism in the tower
when everything that summer afternoon
had slowed right down. But this,

in a room of many windows
and much light, is another silence
palpable, gathered by life's long haul
attempting to do the right thing,
silence waged with thought, and moral.

Don't

Thank you for that word.
It doesn't frighten or appal me,
just the opposite.
It clears vast oceans of
opportunities away,
and leaves me free,
not to. God or someone or
you need to say it to me
more.

A Peculiar Clarity

If I want to hold the silence
to its natural depth, I wait:
wait for the door to bang, the mower
to come to the end of its endless turning,
wait even for clothing to cease to rub
on clothing. Then I wait still more
until the way is clear for the bird
to sing its invisible song,
travelling a long way on the silence,
breaking nothing by its being heard.

Durham Allotments

Professors going to dig their tea
are overlooked in their library of earth
by the Cathedral towers. To me
the whole May scene is held for ever
in a special sort of Saturday afternoon weather.

Skellig Michael: A Pilgrimage

I was on the top of an illuminated wave
the one's you don't believe when you
see them in manuscripts, an upturned 'U',
or on top of a Leviathan, but it was true.
The boat climbed the wave, sat on
top of it, and slid down the other side.
We had the childhood colours too:
blue boat, black sea, white faces.

On arrival the sea doesn't give you up,
but still rolls, and even in your dreams
you will be surging and plummeting,
or leaping off the cliffs like a puffin
which takes a leisurely fifty feet to ease
out of its fall, and tucks its orange feet
behind, and squits its white stuff
like parachutes onto the rocks.

It's only when you leave the lighthouse path
strewn with the skeletons of birds
and thick with a high-pitched smell of bird lime
that you begin to hear the silence
pressing in, far from the engine of the boat
and the orchestrated scream of gulls.

Then the steps begin, the Southern Stairway,
counting six hundred up to an unknown bedroom.
Somehow it felt necessary to be discalced,
my feet, white as a gannet's breast, my boots
hanging round my neck like earrings.
The boatmen I noticed, stayed below.

Rightly, to enter the enclosure you have
to stoop, awkwardly, lowly. You begin by bowing.
In, you cannot see your way out.
The first miracle will be if you're alone,
the second that the sun will shine, the third
that God will talk with you. Pray to St Michael

for three miracles, whose *skellig* it is. Stop.
Breathe. Let in the peace, and if you don't kneel there
where on earth will you kneel?

I looked up and saw an angel standing by the tombs.
She was dressed in brown. She was the guide,
She understood the need for silence.

We can know too much.

This is where the guidebooks stop and the poems begin.
This is where we have to imagine the monks
watching the sky with nothing
between themselves and heaven,
a psalter for food, rain for drink, and possibly
a strip of wheat beyond the enclosure.
This desert is on the edge of the ocean
and they made the edge a virtue.

But surely despair was sometimes the shape
of their beehive hut, a homesickness, when
the elements took leave of God's control
and became something other. Surely, for some,
having said goodbye to the world,
death could not come quickly enough.

A part of us will not come down:
the glimpse of heroism we could never really manage,
a crazy love of Christ, a romance, something
to do with penitence. And as we sit in meetings
in our suits, we'll take the boat again, and climb
with the gulls willing us up further into lightness
for which prayer is the only music, and Christ's coming
the only purpose under heaven.

County Wexford

My shadow lay half the length
of a spinach field. It was that time
of evening, but I turned and walked
back into the sun through the wheat field,
on the tractor tyres' herring-boned path.
Not yet fully ripe the wheat was silver,
like hairs on a summer skin, the whole
swathes of field were smoothed by the wind
stroking the pelt. The wheat succumbed
to the touch as in receipt of gifts. It was then
I noticed other gifts, far off farms in the clefts
of hills, the ascending size of hill to mountain.
In the time it takes for a shadow
to cross a county, I had turned from
onlooker to receiver of bounty.

Autumn in Wivelrod

When talk's of harvest and of God
then autumn's come to Wivelrod.
The blackberry pips lodge in the teeth,
the ferns are wilting in the heat.
The summer's fiercest sun appears,
so that confirms that autumn's here.
O shining, chestnut thoroughbred,
twitching for the mistress-head.
She's gone to school with trunk and rug,
which means, it's Christmas for the hug.
She'll share her dreams with you, and O,
the boy who shared the pedalo.
The lonely biplane in the sky
drones to wish the bees goodbye.
The football shirts are on the line.
The team is back for one more time.
The acorns drop, the beech nuts fall,
I didn't need my coat at all.
I see the brown creeps up the leaf.
I sense an ancient form of grief.

Night Reaping

It doesn't seem right, but that's
the way it is these days. Through
the bedroom window I see stars in flight
dancing up and down the field,
then realise it's the getting of the harvest in.
Stars are headlights.
They are shaving the land by night.
Falling asleep I realise we haven't
a mythology for this, except a dark one:
the grim reaper comes when we least expect it.
But I bet they don't think of that.
It's a job to do, and when I wake
the field is pitted with new black bales, like
flicked ash, and the reapers are in bed, knackered.

The Funeral

(i.m. William Scammell)

So it was to church that you were brought,
at the end of a long road of Sunday mornings
elsewhere, and friends who didn't think it altogether wrong
to honour you in hard, quiet pews came too.
Most of us were strangers to the place.
One came, who loved you, with only just about
her grieving left, orange flowers held against her womb
like a bridesmaid. The deep, wet grave,
at the edge of the churchyard, looked over fields
to the Solway through a faint December light.

There is a place for such occasions then.
You needed to know that it was there:
this sleeping church, with its
organ pipes and pews, pulpit and stained glass,
and your plot of earth, near where you read and wrote
and smoked, and suffered losses like the rest of us.
To all this comforting and clumsy ritual
death committed you, and by your gracious choice
committed me as well. It was in your will
for me to have the final word. After that, we
gathered round in groups to weep or cry, and hug,
and wonder how or why, to reminisce,
awkwardly, or not, or maybe, without you.

The Massacre of the Innocents

(for Sarah, Jessica, Holly and Milly)

This is the only praying
we can do
for the child beyond the reach of us,
beyond the dental records, and the one shoe.

All that is left us is to pray.
Wing our love to the One
who knows the way,
asking for small acts of kindness to be done.

Praying lets the mind's image
dance beyond the pain,
beyond the anxiety of 'finds',
and out of the reach of the rain.

Michelangelo's Rondanini Pietà

It is all still being made
and it is all just breaking up.
He is being carried, and she
is carrying him now. He is bearing up,
and now is carrying her
in such an awkward verticality:
both so tired, so sad. His work
is done: hers, now over, begins again.
The only hope lies in the spring of
knees, which are broken, but ready
for resurrection. The whole world
is on his back, crying 'now!'

Easter (I)

for they were afraid
MARK 16.8

This Easter I shall paint
the walls a Jerusalem colour:
the green hill, the cockerel's crimson throat,
the purple pillar; and time will
fall into hours, the third, the sixth,
the ninth, into ethereal time.
It could be any time as I walk through town,
sensitive yet unbodied, feeling the weight
of the lowering of Christ, and smelling
the sacrificial hot-cross buns.

Why am I so keen to stay with death
and sorrow, so cautious of the light,
and all that yellowness? I am with the women,
falling off the end of the gospel,
afraid. This year I may learn to fall
and not fear, and find myself lifted
to watch the face of forgiveness rise
with such silence and uncanny grace,
that with the thrush, high in the holly tree,
I will sing, *unique...unique...unique.*

Easter (II)

Easter is never a new thing.
It saw the birth of the whole land,
and is present at each slow spring
of a child's five-petalled hand;

At Easter it is Christ we see,
with his hands at their farthest
stretch, hanging on the axle-tree,
nailed to the east and the west.

Easter comes again, at the sign
of the torn heart, for the saddened
company, and the shrivelled vine –
love all alive on the sudden!

Easter (III)

The empty tomb was like a mouth aghast,
all presence gone and so fast. Only clothes
remained, limp like a broken heart.
It lacked all life, no hope could fill the void,
no clues to follow, or hints to clutch at,
not even angels. I have seen men as such.

Yet as the minutes passed, and the thin light
inspired the sparrows and the larks,
I heard a tune that earlier I was deaf to.
Not too early and not too late, before
the dew had dried and in the length
of shadow and of light, I could believe
the tale before ever I was told.
The tomb was empty but my heart was full.
Love pieced together Christ and made him whole.

Resurrection

I think it took her death to do it.
The light that emanated from the space
she left spoke resurrection.
Who she was took hold of time
and turned it inside out,
and the old laughter which took
such toll of pompous hats and dirgy hymns
was transfigured into something
which got under the skin of suffering
and put it in its place.

So now I tell the secret
that resurrection is the glass
through which we see things differently,
and what was first in the mind of God
becomes the truth at last.

Written in Juice of Lemon

Some poems I write in ink
and they get written with a lot
of furrowing of the brow, and often miss
but some I write in juice of lemon
quickly in my heart
and hope that one day someone's
warmth will iron the secrets into poems
with effortless art.